Books by Rachel E. Carr

STEPPING STONES TO JAPANESE FLORAL ART
A YEAR OF FLOWERS
HOURS AND FLOWERS
JAPANESE ART: SYMBOLISM, CULT & PRACTICE
THE JAPANESE WAY WITH FLOWERS
THE PICTURE STORY OF JAPAN

YOGA . . . TODAY! (RECORD ALBUM)

CREATIVE WAYS WITH FLOWERS

RACHEL E. CARR

CREATIVE WAYS WITH FLOWERS

The Best of Two Worlds—
East and West

DOUBLEDAY & COMPANY, INC., GARDEN CITY, NEW YORK

Some of the photographs which appear in this book appeared in *Family Circle* magazine and were taken by George Nordhausen. Other photographs are reprinted with permission of *Home Garden Magazine, The New York Times,* and from *Good Housekeeping,* Copyright © 1969 by the Hearst Corporation, and the booklet, *The Japanese Way with Food and Flowers* (Kikkoman International Inc.)

Library of Congress Catalog Card Number 75–99049

For Persis Gladieux, with love.

Preface

Innumerable books on flower arrangement have already been published. You may well ask how yet another volume on this fascinating subject can be set apart from all others. In this book the floral designs were inspired from the best of two worlds: the Orient and the Occident.

During the years I lived in Japan studying the art of *ikebana*, I discovered the Japanese as the great masters of floral art. With relatively few lines they create strong emotional qualities evoking elements of rhythm, depth, and spirit.

After living in the United States for the past ten years, and having observed the American way with flowers, I have applied the basic principles of Japanese design to floral creations that blend harmoniously with the decor of today's Western living.

You don't need a vast assortment of flower containers. With

a little ingenuity you can devise your own, or make imaginative use of objects that will adapt themselves in texture and form to flower arrangements. Nor do you need masses of flowers. A few used skillfully can be even more effective.

Through the understanding of some basic design principles you will achieve simple yet appealing compositions—as well as dramatic effects—with fresh and dried flowers; even with artificial materials.

The arrangements in this book are not designed to be copied step by step; rather they are inspirational ideas intended to guide and to stimulate your own creativity. With practice you will develop an individual style and experience the delight of self-expression.

RACHEL E. CARR

New York 1969

Contents

CHAPTER 1

Arranging Flowers Is an Art

Arranging flowers is an art similar to painting and sculpturing. When the design is creative it captures the spirit of form with a subtle interplay of relationships in texture and space. A good design is infused with freedom and a degree of control which together bring out the underlying qualities of vitality, rhythm, and depth. Moreover, a good design reflects the arranger's inventiveness and sensitivity.

A well-thought-out design has a theme which can be developed in many ways. For instance: the charm of a particular flower may be evoked showing its blossoms in full view—from bud to maturity, and in varying stages of growth; or a beautiful curved leaf or branch may become the inspiration for the design.

Sometimes the theme may be one of color and texture brought into play to complement the setting of a room. At other times the theme is more obvious; a naturalistic interpretation of nature, or simply a dramatization of form and space in abstract concept.

To achieve success, your flower arrangements should be planned with thought and care. The choice of the container and floral materials will depend on the surroundings in which the arrangement is to be placed. As an example, the modern design in PLATE 36, composed of rich luminous tones using dracaena and carnations in a tan pottery container, is placed in a library setting. The colors and textures used are in pleasing contrast to the handsome leather-bound books on the mahogany table. They also pick up the beige and red colors of the lacquer bowls.

Accessories become a charming addition to a design if they relate well in spirit and form; otherwise the effect is contrived. The two ebony cranes used in *Figure 60* with soft green ferns and pink geraniums seem to belong to the woodland and appear to be enjoying their reflections in the mirrored base.

To achieve depth, movement, and height, keep your designs simple. You can create a composition of simplicity and quiet charm with only a few flowers, such as the three roses in PLATE 11. The framework is an asymmetric, or uneven triangle—one of the basic principles of Japanese design. Each flower is in a different stage of growth and height. The tallest rose is given a backward slant, the rose to the right is slightly forward, and the shortest one in front slants to the left. This creates depth. White marble chips that artfully conceal the needlepoint holder give the arrangement a finishing touch. The principle of this basic framework is repeated in many of the arrangements illustrated.

Another example of the flexible triangle is applied to the colorful composition of anemones in PLATE 17. Notice how the two separate groupings form individual triangles in two black lacquer bowls lined with yellow. The containers are staggered, almost touching, so that the flowers and leather ferns, which emerge from the separate groups, interrelate to form a complete triangular design. A sense of arrested motion is expressed by the sway of the flowers and leaves. White marble chips cover the needlepoint holders to heighten the design.

In abstract compositions let your imagination have free rein, but keep in mind the formulas of good design. In *Figure 38* slender looped bulrushes, which create kinetic energy and tension, repeat the serpentine form of the pale green pottery container as they spiral upward to the vertical reeds kept tautly together. For impact and contrast a rising creamy white calla lily and two shorter ones are added at the base.

ELEMENTARY TECHNIQUES

Knowledge of some elementary techniques will develop your skill in arranging flowers. The best support for a shallow container is the needlepoint holder shown in *Figure A*. These come in various sizes and shapes. If branch ends of the floral materials are cut at a slant they will rest securely in the holder, and will also absorb water more freely.

Figure A.

When a branch is too heavy for the holder, press a strip of florist clay around the rim of the holder so it will adhere to the container. (Do this before adding water so the clay will not become slippery in the container.) Sometimes a rock or two added near the holder will support the weight of heavier branches and conceal the holder. Small pebbles over and around the holder, or short foliage, are other ways of screening it.

A needlepoint holder is usually not used in tall vases because of the depth; these require different techniques to balance the floral materials within the upper part of the container. Two types are illustrated: the Y-support in *Figure B* and the cross-support in *Figure C*.

To make a Y-support, use a thick straight branch about half

an inch in diameter. Cut it to measure almost the height of the vase. Split the tip about two inches down (to insert floral materials in it). Cut the bottom end straight so it will rest flat in the base of the vase. This support is used generally for a tall, narrow vase.

Figure B.

Figure C.

For a wider shaped vase, make a cross-support. Use two sturdy branches about half an inch in diameter cut to measure across the container, just below the rim. Make diagonal cuts on the ends, cross the branches, and tie them securely with florist wire. The support should fit tightly into the vase with the diagonal ends pressing against the sides of the vase, so the materials will balance securely in any of the four spaces. If the ends of branches and flowers are cut at a slant, they will rest against the walls of the container. This ensures further support.

Techniques for dried and artificial flowers differ from those adapted to fresh materials, and are dealt with specifically in Chapters 6 and 7.

PLATE 1. An ordinary bread basket lends a rustic appeal to a simple arrangement of yellow chrysanthemums and aralia leaves.

PLATE 2. This informal arrangement contrasts the movement and depth of various zinnias against the vertical strength of Scotch broom.

PLATE 3. Marigolds and springeri in a narrow container can add charm
to a patio, kitchen or breakfast table.

PLATE 4. Almost anything can be turned into an attractive flower container. Here geraniums are displayed in an ordinary baking pan.

PLATE 5. By spraying the pan and wrapping it in twine, a mundane utensil has been made into an unusual and decorative container.

PLATE 6. Slats of stained wood have been nailed around a rectangular baking pan to set off these yellow gladioli perfectly.

PLATE 7. A serving platter of pottery holds a single Easter lily and massed acacia.

PLATE 8. Curving bittersweet branches dramatize the flat plane of the container, but make its vivid coral an integral part of the design.

PLATE 9. When using a shallow container, a feeling of depth can be conveyed by filling it with water, or by spreading short sprays around the base. Here sprigs of cypress foliage strengthen orange chrysanthemums.

PLATE 10. Plastic bowl with lid is a useful container for impromptu arrangements.

PLATE 11. The basic round bowl is an essential part of a flower arranger's collection.

BASIC EQUIPMENT

A flower arranger's basic equipment should consist of the following:

1/ Pair of sharp flower scissors to cut heavy branches.
2/ Wire clippers to cut artificial stems.
3/ Various sizes of needlepoint holders.
4/ Cage holders for artificial flowers.
5/ Florist wire, clay, and tape.
6/ Pebbles and rocks of different sizes, colors, textures, and shapes.
7/ Water spray to freshen arrangements (any atomizer attached to a bottle will do).

Keep your equipment in a special place within easy reach.

CHOICE OF FLOWER CONTAINERS

Flower containers are an essential part of good arrangements and the right one will heighten interest in a design. Avoid ornamental vases and bowls which are finished art objects in themselves and compete with the flower arrangement.

Your basic collection should include simple round, oval, square, rectangular, and cylindrical shapes. The textures and colors should vary from dull finishes to high glosses. Beige, green, black, white, and brown are colors that blend well with most floral materials.

SOME HELPFUL POINTERS

When selecting your flowers and foliage, pick them in early stages of growth for two reasons: they will last longer and you can enjoy their gradual development after they have been arranged.

Cut plants in the early morning while the dew is still fresh, or in the evening after sundown. As a conditioning process submerge the materials in a bucket of deep cool water for at least two hours.

After you have made your selection of the container and floral materials, prepare your work table so all your equipment is within easy reach. You will be able to create with greater ease and pleasure if there is soft music in the background to inspire your mood and to relax you. Take your time when arranging flowers. Don't rush. Study the shape and curve of each flower and branch before placing it in the container. Look for the most appealing lines and use those to contribute to a design. If blossoms appear overcrowded, remove a few. Do the same with the leaves, but prune with care so as not to snip off the desirable lines.

First build the framework of your design, then add the supplementary lines. Finally, put in the finishing touches by covering the mechanics that support the floral materials, and spray the completed arrangement with a fine mist of cool water.

The easiest way to replenish water in a container is to use a syringe to draw out the stale water, then pour in a fresh supply, filling the container to the rim. Your arrangements will last longer if you avoid a sunny or drafty area.

You are now on your way to creative designing with flowers, an art you will enjoy anywhere at anytime as a form of self-expression.

CHAPTER 2

Improvised Containers

Selecting a suitable container for a specific setting requires thought. Even though you may possess a variety of containers, the one right for a chosen environment may be missing. With a little ingenuity you can improvise flower containers from bottles, boxes, bread baskets, baking pans, serving platters, and other adaptable forms. The scope is endless. With modest skill you can make containers out of copper, plumber's lead, porous rock, and wood.

Bread baskets, for example, lend rustic appeal to informal arrangements for a patio, kitchen, or breakfast table. A needle-point holder in a small can of water will secure the flowers and foliage and keep them fresh.

In PLATE 1, a cluster of yellow chrysanthemums framed by two wide aralia leaves nestle low in the center for an all-round view. Small blossoms fill in for depth. The needlepoint holder is concealed by the extended rim of the basket.

The same basket is used in PLATE 2 for an entirely different composition. Colorful zinnias of varying heights and directions create motion and depth for the strong vertical lines of Scotch broom. Thick leaves around the blossoms were pruned for airiness in design; overlapping short foliage serves to blanket the needlepoint holder.

Masses of garden flowers, such as marigolds, have an affinity for the rustic textured basket in PLATE 3. Touches of springeri break the monotony of massed blossoms in the narrow container. The appeal of this centerpiece lies in its free and natural form.

Baking pans in simple shapes—round, square, or rectangular —can be disguised by spraying with lacquer paint, wrapping with twine, or bordering with wood.

The round baking pan in PLATE 4 was sprayed red, then wrapped with twine. To prevent the twine from raveling, after the first strand has been wound around the pan into place, put a coating of glue on each succeeding strand. The result, a rustic container for bright red geraniums which are arranged to heighten their natural manner of growth.

The same container is used in PLATE 5, with fresh pussy willows individually shaped to give rhythmic motion to the low grouping of red camellias. Glossy leaves which spread over the needlepoint holder cover it skillfully, at the same time providing a feeling of depth.

The rectangular baking pan in PLATE 6 becomes the lining for a wood container. After the pan was sprayed dark brown, stained mahogany wood slats were glued to the pan's walls with the ends extending. Invisible nails reinforce the framework at the joints. This container holds three tall stalks of yellow gladioli with leather ferns to soften their rigid lines. Brown pebbles drift into the open water with a few banked over the needlepoint holder.

Wine bottles, which come in an assortment of shapes, textures, and colors can be used effectively for flower arrangements. Two examples are shown in *Figures* 1 and 2. The bottles them-

Figures 1–2. Wine bottles make ideal containers since their narrow necks require no mechanical aids to support flowers or branches.

Figure 3. A large round platter serves as a container for this woodland creation.

selves have a unique vase-like quality; their narrow necks require no mechanical aids to support the flowers or branches.

The slender blue glass bottle holds wisteria tendrils that swirl around two red roses and leather ferns in an airy, rhythmic effect. The color of the flowers is repeated in the lacquered plywood base. (To make the base, cut half-inch-thick plywood into three pieces: a diamond and two triangles. These can be arranged into different geometric forms for various compositions. The base shown here was lacquered orange-red on one side and black on the other.)

Rich textures of the brown pottery bottle complement a bronze-colored anthurium, which stands out sharply against wispy Italian wheat and reddish-brown geranium foliage. A symphony of muted tones is the mood for this design.

Round and oval serving platters adapt to versatile use in floral designs. If they are too shallow for water, a needlepoint holder in a small can will support the floral materials. The holder can be disguised with foliage, rocks, or pebbles.

In *Figure* 3 yellow and red Duchess chrysanthemums make an appealing double composition in a black plastic platter. Leather ferns, added for depth, and a scatter of small stones help to conceal the holders.

A coral pottery platter becomes the container for three different arrangements. In PLATE 7 the platter is filled with water to create an illusion of depth for aspidistra leaves furled to encircle a solitary Easter lily with massed acacia centered low. Two rocks, different in size and shape, conceal the cup holder. (To furl leaves such as aspidistra, roll the tip around a slender pencil, then rub briskly between heels of the palms until the furl takes shape.)

In PLATE 8 the same leaves are used again for a low arrangement with tall bittersweet branches to form the outline. Short sprays of bittersweet berries, spread over the cup holder, provide depth, and white pebbles which drift into the platter add a note of accent to the design.

Fresh, flexible pussy willows adapt themselves to a variety of graceful forms. In PLATE 9 they are looped to create a whirling movement for a centerpiece with bronze chrysanthemums which contrast well with an orange platter. Sprigs of cypress foliage are spread around the flowers for depth. (The loops are made by tying the tips and ends together with florist wire. Willow when dried can be used indefinitely, and the loops become a permanent outline for other creative arrangements.)

The unique container in *Figure* 4 is a lava rock with a natural crevice. The sharp edges were filed down to produce a smooth surface, and the crevice lined with copper.

To emphasize the rich textural quality of the rock, the floral composition is stark and simple. Slender branches of bridal wreath seem to grow in different levels behind a thick short branch which simulates a tree trunk. Three candlestick lilies, grouped low, complete the symbolic triangle. Close inspection reveals dark pebbles scattered over the needlepoint holder, blending naturally into the color of the copper lining.

Bowls of simple shapes and boxes which hold water make ideal containers for impromptu arrangements.

A round bowl of black plastic becomes a centerpiece with

Figure 4. The
unique container is a
lava rock with a
natural crevice,
lined with copper.

its lid tilted against a base of black oval glass in PLATE 10.
Airy pine branches form the framework. The taller branch ac-
tually leans at a low angle to give an all-round view with the tip
turning inward to counterbalance the shorter branch. In the
center, fragile cyclamen blossoms nestle amid their leaves, some
of which are spread out naturally to furnish dimension. The
needlepoint holder is concealed by the tilted lid.

In *Figure 5* a black plastic box holds two mauve Dutch
irises combined with sword-shaped leaves. Pink geraniums, which
are arranged in a low cluster, provide depth and contrast to
the vigorous lines of the irises and leaves. Interest is added to
the design by the tilted lid across the box, which also helps
to conceal the needlepoint holder. (The same container is used
in *Figure 24.*)

The brass watering can in *Figure 6* is an example of an
adaptable object picked at random for a flower container. The
can holds an exotic pink cactus orchid silhouetted by the
velvet softness of mint geraniums. Its graceful brass form is
accentuated by the black oval lacquer base.

Figure 5. (right) A plastic box, simulating lacquer, becomes a container for this iris and geranium design.

Figure 6. (below) The brass watering can is an example of an adaptable object picked at random for use as a flower container.

CHAPTER 3

Versatile Basic Shapes

Flower containers of basic shapes—round, square, oval, rectangular, and cylindrical—adapt well to different arrangements. When the color of the container is monochromatic with subtle textural overtones, its understated simplicity will blend with floral materials.

The basic round bowl is an essential part of any collection. It can vary in form, texture, and color.

In PLATE 11 the transparent red glass bowl holds three roses that repeat a similar shade of red. Arranged in varying stages of development and height, the flowers rise in simple charm from a bed of marble chips.

A similar design is expressed in the blue porcelain bowl of PLATE 12, with seven pink carnations in a lacery of baby's breath to provide dimensional softness. In studying the design, you will notice that the carnations form a triangle.

The red pottery bowl in PLATE 13 contrasts dramatically

with a composition of aspidistra leaves whose interrelated lines flow rhythmically. Two furled leaves break the monotony of the same directional movement, and white stones accent the starkly simple design.

Compotes have always been popular for arranging flowers because of their simple, yet varying shapes.

Figures 7–9 are identically shaped containers but different in color and texture. The swirl in the mottled black compote is a foil to conceal the needlepoint holder. The rough texture of the container intensifies the beauty of red and pink carnations merged with airy asparagus ferns in a free and natural composition. (*Figure 7*)

Beauty in design is often achieved by a sparse use of materials. A white magnolia stands out against clearly defined red-bud blossoms and pine sprays in a white mottled compote; its opaque quality lends distinction to the floral materials. (*Figure 8*)

The compote, in glossy jade green, blends agreeably with looped wisteria tendrils (each tip tied with wire to its base), which form the framework for yellow chrysanthemums and croton leaves. (*Figure 9*)

Another set of identically shaped containers, each different in color and texture, is illustrated in *Figures 10–12*.

The compote of matte finish sandalwood holds an abstract pattern of bent equisetum (horsetails) that is in forceful opposition to the large yellow chrysanthemum. (*Figure 10*)

A sweeping line of variegated aspidistra extends sharply beyond the glossy midnight blue compote, with shorter leaves to counterbalance the framework. In the center a tight cluster of red carnations nestles snugly among the foilage. The smooth textures of the floral materials are in harmony with the container placed on a marble coffee table. (*Figure 11*)

The same floral materials and container shown in *Figure 11* are used again in an entirely different composition. Three aspidistra leaves are loosely looped in a centerpiece with short red carnations that weave in and out of the framework. (*Figure 12*)

When creating large arrangements, or woodland and water scenes, rectangular and oval shapes are best to achieve spatial

Figures 7–9. These identically shaped compote containers are different only in color and texture. Each is used with a totally different creation to show its adaptability.

Figures 10–12. Another example of an adaptable compote shape. *Figures* 11–12 are centerpieces using the same striped aspidistra and carnations.

balance. Some examples are shown in *Figures* 13–15 and Plate 14.

Fresh daisies, arborvitae foliage with pine sprigs become a woodland scene for a rectangular container made of rosewood. The voids are linked by balanced spacing between high and low levels. Rocks and pebbles which conceal the needlepoint holders bring out the charm of this naturalistic composition. (*Figure* 13)

A scenic landscape is created with a blueberry branch, yellow Dutch irises, and mugho pine in an oval bronze-colored container of porcelain. Brown and beige pebbles which drift in the container add a pleasing touch to this earthy composition. (*Figure* 14)

The same oval form in a satin black finish harmonizes with the smooth textures of New Zealand flax individually looped and tied with florist wire to form a centerpiece outline for massed clivia of deep orange. (*Figure* 15)

Typical of Japanese symbolic designs, this simulated pond scene in Plate 14 of irises, water lilies, and reeds portrays the past, present, and future. Movement in the design is created by the fragile nature of reeds, which seem to sway in the wind; some are sharply bent to indicate the past. Open blossoms express the present, while buds hold promise for the future. Water lily pads skillfully conceal the separate needlepoint holders. This satisfying naturalistic composition in a blue porcelain container gives lasting pleasure.

The technique of regrouping iris leaves to dramatize them in an arrangement is a worthwhile study. Separate the clump, rub each leaf on both sides with a wet cloth, then regroup the leaves in twos and threes (in different height groupings) with their tips pointing inward. This is the way they grow.

A half-circle container is highly versatile. Its curve can be turned to the front, reversed; or two identical shapes may be paired or staggered. Plates 15–16, and *Figures* 16–17 are good examples, as well as *Figures* 22 and 59.

The red container in Plate 15 contrasts dynamically with yellow daisies and mugho pine, which reflect a natural woodland scene.

PLATE 12. The bowl may vary in size, color, and shape, but it should always be integrated into the complete arrangement.

PLATE 13. The red pottery container provides dramatic contrast with the aspidistra leaves, accented by white chips.

PLATE 14. Rectangular containers give interesting spatial balance to a double arrangement as in this pond scene.

PLATE 15. The versatility of the half-circle container is demonstrated in this woodland scene of yellow daisies and mugo pine.

PLATE 16. With curve reversed, the container gives dramatic emphasis to the harmony of a high and low level.

PLATE 17. Twin black lacquer bowls, lined with yellow, form compositional unity for anemones and leather ferns.

PLATE 18. Twin wood containers are staggered in a landscape for a weeping willow and Dutch irises with foliage.

PLATE 19. A starkly modern design with double-tiered containers using onion heads in contrast to a jet of gladioli.

Plate 20. Ti leaves rise in overlapping lines from the lower tier of chrysanthemums in the upper tier, with pine as an effective link.

PLATE 21. Two tiers of an antique Chinese basket are filled with pink geraniums in a natural, free style.

Figure 13. A handmade container of rosewood holds a woodland atmosphere. Its rectangular shape gives the necessary spatial balance.

Figures 14–15. Oval containers provide adequate area space for designs such as the woodland scene using a blueberry branch with Dutch irises and pine, and the centerpiece with New Zealand flax and clivia.

In PLATE 16 the curve is reversed in the ivory-colored container for a double composition emphasizing high and low levels. There is a harmonious relationship between the tall smooth blue Dutch irises streaked with yellow and low clusters of mauve heather.

The same ivory-colored container with the curve in front is used in a composition of simple charm. In *Figure* 16 a sharp bend in one pandanus leaf gives strong accent to three deep mauve Dutch irises, their yellow streaks adding a note of interest.

Smooth and rough textures fuse agreeably in the satin black container of *Figure* 17, which holds two cycas fern palms, with one emphatically curved for rhythm. The palms lend their strong character to shell pink anthuriums. Short pine unobtrusively covers the needlepoint holder.

There are certain settings in a home where a tall vase would be more appropriate than a shallow container. Since tall vase designs are more difficult to arrange than those in shallow containers, different techniques are described in Chapter 1.

In *Figures* 18–19 the interesting swirl shape of the vase gives a design originality. The vase, in glossy black, brings out harmonious overtones of color and texture in the composition. Corkscrew willow creates an illusion of depth and weightlessness in the background for colorful anemones arranged in interesting counterbalances. The support used is a cross-fixture.

In mottled white, a vase of the same shape changes character and is in pleasing monochromatic concord with white cherry blossoms interspersed with pine. The same cross-fixture is used.

Figures 16–17. The white and black half-circle containers of the same shape illustrate what can be done in different floral designs when imagination is put to use.

Figures 18–19. The same swirl vase appears in a satiny black
finish with corkscrew willow and anemones; and in a rough
white texture with cherry blossoms and pine.

CHAPTER 4

Emphasis on Compositional Unity

To give spirit and unity to floral compositions when more than one container is used calls for imagination and an understanding of interrelationships of form and space. The harmonious placement of the containers and compatible floral materials are also important.

Two or more containers of identical form may be used, or different but related shapes, such as a vase and a bowl.

In PLATE 17 twin black lacquer bowls lined with yellow contrast well with the double airy composition of colorful anemones. The containers are staggered, almost touching, so that the flowers and leather ferns, which emerge from the two separate groups, interrelate to form a complete triangular design. A sense of arrested motion is expressed by the sway of the flowers and leaves. White marble chips cover the needlepoint holders to heighten the design.

In *Figure* 20 two pottery bowls of vibrant red—one larger than the other—are contrasted by a subdued design of fragile Japanese white irises enveloped by their narrow blades. The separate high and low groups in different stages of growth appear to rise from beds of white marble chips and impart an illusion of strong unity between the flowers and the bowls.

The mood changes in *Figure* 21, using the same red bowls with white irises and pale pink water lilies in a design reflecting the natural habitat of plants which grow near each other. Water lily pads conceal the three small needlepoint holders securing the blossoms.

Two half-circle containers in *Figure* 22 are staggered to reproduce a woodland scene. Pine boughs and star lilies seem to lean across a bank, and their reflection is caught in the clear pool of water. Covering the needlepoint holders is a gnarled piece of circular driftwood which strides across the two containers to link them into compositional unity.

Rectangular-shaped containers have many possibilities. They can be used as a pair, staggered, or placed one on top of the other to provide spatial balance and freedom of expression.

The twin wood containers in PLATE 18 are staggered in a landscape setting for a tall willow whose wispy limbs flow downward, as though moving in a breeze. Dutch irises, boxwood, and begonia foliage are combined in a sparse grouping to accentuate the quiet, reflective mood of a wooded atmosphere.

The aquamarine containers in *Figure* 23 give unusual interest to linear pear branches which rise from extreme ends of a double-tiered composition. Pale pink peonies, arranged low, unite the groups and stand out in etched clarity.

The starkly modern design in PLATE 19 is a subtle blending of textural harmony with the modern painting. Exotic onion heads are in direct contrast to a jet of pink gladioli arranged in grayish-green pottery containers, placed one on top of the other. The color combinations in the floral design echo those found in the painting.

In PLATE 20 ti leaves rise in overlapping lines from the lower tier to meet deep red chrysanthemums massed in a ball of the upper tier. The containers are black lacquer. Short pine

Figures 20–21. The same red pottery bowls are used effectively in pond-like studies: one of Japanese white irises alone, and the other a combination of the irises with pale pink water lilies.

sprigs which conceal the needlepoint holders provide an effective link for this modern design.

Figure 24 is a good example of how a waterproof box can serve as a two-tiered container. Placed on an end table, the design consists of three staggered conium stalks which rise closely erect from the lower tier; a pale yellow dahlia appears to float in the inverted lid placed across the box.

Certain flowers, like the rich florets of geraniums and their strong textured leaves, are best arranged in a natural and free style. In PLATE 21 two tiers of an antique Chinese basket are filled with a bouquet of pink geraniums. The feeling is of studied casualness.

A tall vase and a shallow bowl can be effectively combined into a double arrangement if they unite agreeably in form, color, and texture. For example, in PLATE 22 white camellias are used to grace a slender yellow glass vase and matching bowl. Wisteria tendrils, which are wrapped around the vase and flow downward into the bowl, merge into compositional unity. No mechanics are needed for the slender vase since the floral materials balance securely within its narrow neck. A needlepoint holder secures the flowers and wisteria in the bowl.

In the lyrical scene of PLATE 23, an ebony crane stands near a concealed bowl amid tall blue Dutch irises and a low bed of red geraniums. Smooth black pebbles link bowl and a tall, handmade container that simulates a bridge and holds fluffy onion heads.

The spirit of bold adventure is given form by masses of fresh green maple and a dynamic wisteria branch that leaps out of a sculptured pale green vase in *Figure 25*. To balance the open spaces, perky daisies and sprigs of maple, in a small bowl of matching color and texture, peer from behind the vase. Maple branches are supported by the sturdy wisteria, and daisies by a small needlepoint holder.

Rustic miniature bridges, when part of a floral design, create a scenic interpretation as shown in *Figure 26*. Irises and wisteria boughs rise above the wooden bridges. Sprigs of mugho pine, rocks and pebbles are added to create further realism, and at the same time concealing the mechanics.

The wooden bridges measure twenty-eight inches long, six and a half inches wide, and five and a half inches high. Round notches, under the bridges, secure the legs.

A modern, illusionary landscape in PLATE 24 is created by the use of small black porcelain containers staggered on a buffet against a background of jet black glass. The flowers are white irises, conium stalks, and yellow button chrysanthemums. Black sand covers the individual needlepoint holders.

Figure 22. A gnarled driftwood strides across two half-circle red containers to reproduce a woodland scene with pine boughs and star lilies.

Figure 23. The aquamarine porcelain containers form a double-tiered composition for linear pear branches and pink peonies.

Figure 24. A black plastic box serves as a double tier for conium stalks and a pale yellow dahlia on an end table.

Figure 25. The spirit of bold adventure is given form by masses of green maple, a dynamic wisteria branch, and perky daisies in a pale green pottery vase and matching bowl.

Figure 26. Irises and wisteria boughs rise above rustic miniature bridges in a scenic composition.

CHAPTER 5

A Medley of Ideas

The ideas conveyed in this chapter fall into specific categories. They are Emphasis on Framework, Decorative Wall Themes, Accent on Woody Forms, Beauty at Random, and Play on Leaves.

EMPHASIS ON FRAMEWORK

A practical method of creating the framework of a design is to use long-lasting branches. Then flowers can be changed or renewed at any time without destroying the structural outline. Such a frame can also be created from dried branches of rhythmic quality.

In PLATE 25 well-trimmed laurel branches form a basic design in a white porcelain bowl. To create depth the taller branch leans slightly backward, and the shorter one forward. Centered low is a triangle of short-stemmed gladioli with sprigs of cedar to fill in the open gaps and to cover the needlepoint holder. The off-center arrangement adds interest.

When a branch is used as a symbolic tree in a landscape scene, it should have the appearance of growing naturally as does the tall mountain pine in *Figure 27*. The pine needles are spread at different levels to create movement, depth, and height. Arranged low are red and white trillium lilies combined with leather ferns. The flowers do not overpower the pine, but become an intrinsic part of the design. To contribute to this woodland effect, and help counterbalance the heavy branch, two rocks are banked near the needlepoint holder in an oval white pottery container.

In the arrangement shown in *Figure 28*, a clearly defined camellia branch reaches out in distinct levels from a white porcelain vase and adds height and depth to the low masses of orange clivia. An orange tone, similar to that of the blossoms, is picked up by the half-circle bases.

Linear movement is frequently achieved by the rhythmic qualities of natural curves such as the bare whirling forms of the wisteria vine in PLATE 26. This has sufficient melodic movement to create strong interest in a simple composition with bright red geraniums. Soft spreading leaves at the base camouflage the needlepoint holder in the earthy greenish-brown container.

A totally different feeling is carried out by dried wisteria vine which floats naturally around the slender porcelain vase of satiny black finish in *Figure 29*. Delicate bridal wreath frames a pale pink peony inserted in a Y-support.

In *Figure 30* the forceful natural line of a cotoneaster branch sweeps across a sleek black porcelain compote and provides dynamic contrast to a tight cluster of red carnations. Short mugho pine sprigs add depth and cover the needlepoint holder. (A similar line can be reproduced with pliant branches of Scotch broom or pussy willow.)

DECORATIVE WALL THEMES

A blank wall or niche can be given a decorative touch by a hanging flower arrangement. To emphasize the downward flow-

Figure 27. Tall mountain pine, trillium lilies, and leather ferns create a landscape scene in a white pottery container.

Figure 28. A clearly defined camellia branch is combined with massed orange clivia in a white porcelain vase, placed on half-circle orange bases.

Figure 29. Dried wisteria vine unites with a pale pink peony and bridal wreath in a porcelain vase of satiny black.

ing lines of such a design, the container should be suspended above eye level. Containers may vary in shape and texture from openwork baskets to rustic buckets or cylindrical shapes.

The openwork basket in PLATE 27 is attached to a wooden plaque. A narrow bottle holds water for the hanging ivy and bright anemones. They are supported in a cross-fixture. Long-lasting ivy makes a durable framework, and a succession of flowers provide changing centers of interest.

A similar basket and wall plaque are used with a framework of pussy willows in PLATE 28. The pliant fresh stems of willow can be shaped into any form; when dried they last indefinitely. To accentuate the downward flow of the lines, sparse red roses with touches of mugho pine are added as a counterbalance and provide a subtle interplay of textures.

For a rustic note on a patio, a hanging bucket made of weathered wood gives a pleasing touch. A needlepoint cup holder supports the sinuous downward curves of wisteria tendrils in PLATE 29, providing an off-center frame for deep red garden roses and leather ferns.

ACCENT ON WOODY FORMS

Driftwood, dried limbs, bleached or peeled branches can be used imaginatively in naturalistic or abstract creations.

For example, the gnarled stump used in PLATE 30 becomes a symbolic tree trunk for a tall nandina branch with an umbrella-like spread. Concealed behind the stump is a needlepoint cup holder which supports the nandina. Two cymbidium orchids, mugho pine, and dried sumac are added in pleasing harmony to the woodland, the whole placed on a large burl slab.

In *Figure 31* rich textures of a dried oak branch covered with lichen intensify a tall earthenware vase on a burl slab. To balance the simple design are two giant bronze chrysanthemums with a cluster of boxwood placed low in front. A cross-support secures the oak branch, whose limbs, spread in two dimension, give the design height and depth.

Figure 30. A cotoneaster branch sweeps across a black porcelain compote and provides dynamic contrast to red carnations and mugho pine.

Figure 31. A dried oak branch with lichen merges with giant chrysanthemums and boxwood in an earthenware vase on a burl slab.

Figure 32 shows a distinctive modern design composed of two peeled upside down edgeworthia branches which balance each other in a greenish-brown pottery container splashed with yellow. The emphatic vertical lines of the fork-shaped branches are interwoven with fresh pine sprays and yellow chrysanthemums that echo the colors of the container. A needlepoint holder supports the materials.

A study of contrasts is expressed in *Figure* 33. Abounding with movement is the serpentine form of the curved driftwood which winds its way up and around a narrow black mottled vase. From it, in an airy background of springeri ferns, rise two striking birds of paradise. The floral materials get their support from the driftwood, which dips into the vase.

BEAUTY AT RANDOM

There are times when artlessness in design brings out the natural beauty of flowers, as in PLATES 31–32. Deep red geraniums are casually arranged in an openwork basket for a patio table. The flowers are supported in a needlepoint cup holder. Orange clustered snowballs are massed in an all-round centerpiece. Note how the circular form and color of the pottery bowl harmonize with the flowers.

PLAY ON LEAVES

Arranging a few flowers with their foliage can be dramatic, particularly if the flowers have strong textural appeal. A good example is the iris design in *Figure* 34. The open blossom shows off its fragile mauve petals in contrast to a tight bud. The flowers are surrounded, as they grow, by their strap leaves. They are in pleasing harmony with the stark white porcelain bowl; its swirl is a perfect guise for the needlepoint holder.

Clusters of pink cyclamen appear to be growing naturally out of a white pottery bowl in *Figure* 35. The low spread of its foliage blankets the base.

Figure 36 is a design of understated simplicity: the setting, a long mahogany table in a hallway. A slender magnolia branch sweeps outward from the brown pottery compote in sharp contrast to the opulent texture of a white magnolia blossom and bud. Shorter magnolia foliage spreads low around the base.

Figure 37 shows a handmade wood container, lacquered black. It holds resilient leaves of the bird of paradise, which encircle their exotic orange and blue wax-like flowers in a triangular design of simplicity.

GEOMETRIC PATTERNS

Humble wild reeds hold a treasure of ideas for abstract creations. In *Figure* 38 looped slender bulrushes in kinetic energy and tension, repeat the serpentine form of the pale green pottery container as they spiral upward to the tall reeds kept tautly together. For impact and contrast, a rising creamy white calla lily is added with two shorter blossoms at the base. (The loops are formed by making sharp bends in the single reeds. Each loop is placed in the needlepoint holder directly behind the rising grouped reeds to create a spiral effect.)

Bulrushes are looped to repeat the egg-shaped contour of a black and white porcelain container in *Figure* 39. The needlepoint holder is concealed by three large-spathed white calla lilies cradled in the center to give strong emphasis to the design. (The reeds were grouped in three separate clumps of different heights. Each group was tied with fine wire at tip and base, then the individual reeds were pulled to form loose loops.)

Sharply bent bulrushes in *Figure* 40 create a design of interesting counterbalances for a tight cluster of red carnations in a modern container of pale green pottery. Its harp-like shape is repeated by the reeds. The carnations completely conceal the needlepoint holder.

Figure 32. Fork-shaped edgeworthia branches interweave with fresh pine sprays and yellow chrysanthemums in a greenish-brown pottery container splashed with yellow.

Figure 33. A serpentine of curved driftwood winds its way up and around a black mottled vase to meet birds of paradise in a filmy background of springeri ferns.

Figure 34. In a white porcelain bowl, the fragile mauve petals of a bearded iris and bud stand out in etched clarity surrounded, as they grow, by their strap leaves.

Figure 35. Clusters of pink cyclamen appear to be growing naturally out of a white pottery bowl.

Figure 36. The understated simplicity of this magnolia arrangement in a brown pottery compote graces a long mahogany table in a hallway.

Figure 37. The black-lacquered L-shaped container holds resilient leaves of the bird of paradise, which encircle their exotic
flowers in a triangular design.

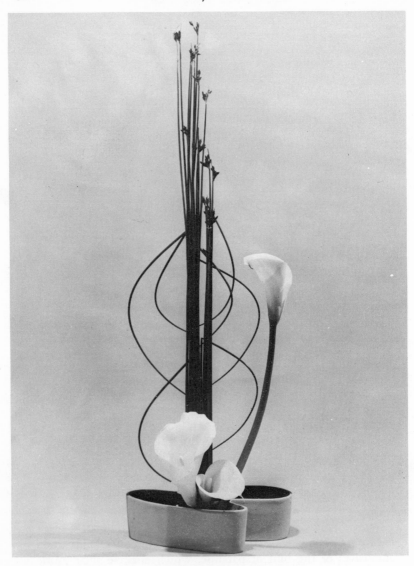

Figures 38–40. Geometric designs with bulrushes, each abstract in concept. In *Figure 38 (above)* looped reeds repeat the serpentine form of the pottery container and are in sharp contrast to the calla lilies. In *Figure 39 (top right)* reeds are looped to repeat the egg-shaped contour of the container with three calla lilies cradled in the center. In *Figure 40 (lower right)* sharply bent loops of reeds create interesting counterbalances for the cluster of red carnations in a harp-like container.

CHAPTER 6

Dried Flowers with a Fresh Look

Wild flowers and ornamental grasses, a changing pageant of the fields, meadows, and roadside, can be dried successfully by an amateur. It is a rewarding hobby that provides a profusion of dried materials the year round.

Drying flowers naturally is a simple process. Hang them upside down in loose bunches in a dark area with good air circulation for ten days to two weeks. This will completely dehydrate the plants. A list of the flowers and foliage that can be dried in this manner is given on page 65.

To achieve a supple bronze texture for leaves, try the glycerin method—a process which usually takes about three weeks. Clean the leaves with a damp cloth, then crush the branch or stem end for about two inches, or make deep slits before placing it in a solution of *one part glycerin to two parts water.*

PLATE 22. White camellia blossoms and wisteria tendrils arranged in a vase and bowl unite into pleasing compositional unity.

PLATE 23. Dutch irises and geraniums with onion heads are combined in a lyrical scene complemented by an ebony crane.

PLATE 24. Irises, conium stalks, and button chrysanthemums combine well in an illusionary landscape.

PLATE 25. Laurel branches form the structural outline for gladioli and cedar placed off-center in a porcelain bowl.

PLATE 26. The bare whirling form of wisteria creates interest for the geraniums in an earthy container.

PLATE 27. An openwork basket on a wall plaque holds trailing ivy and colorful anemones.

PLATE 28. A similar basket and wall plaque are used with a framework of pussy willows and sparse roses with pine.

PLATE 29. A hanging bucket of weathered wood with trailing vine and garden roses gives a pleasing rustic note to a patio.

PLATE 30. A gnarled stump becomes a tree trunk for nandina, with cymbidium orchids, pine, and sumac in a woody scene.

(Some flower driers use an even proportion of glycerin and water.) Place in a dark area. During the treatment the leaves begin to change in color from tan to dark brown, depending on the plant's absorption of glycerin and the length of time it is left in the solution. The plants which respond to this method are listed on page 66.

A wide selection of dried flowers is available commercially. Some, such as cecropia leaves, sea oats, wheat, barley, artichoke heads, sky rockets, thistle, yarrow, cockscomb, and dock are dyed in an assortment of colors.

HANG AND DRY METHOD

Acacia	Fountain Grass	Pandanus
Agapanthus	Gaillardia	Pepper Grass
Alfalfa	Globe Thistle	Pussy Willow
Aralia	Goldenrod	Queen Anne's Lace
Artichoke	Heather	Sansevieria
Astilbe	Heavenly Bamboo	Sea Oats
Baby's Breath	Holly	Seed Pods
Bells-of-Ireland	Leek	Sky Rockets
Bittersweet	Lily Pods	Spirea
Broom Sedge	Love Apples	Statice
Castor Bean	Lunaria	Strawflowers
Cattails	Marigold	Sumac
Chinese Lantern	Milkweed Pods	Thistle
Cockscomb	New Zealand Flax	Weeds
Corn Tassels	Oak	Wheat
Cycas Fern Palm	Oat Grass	Wild Grasses
Dock	Okra	Wisteria Vine
Edgeworthia	Onion	Yarrow
Eucalyptus	Pampas Grass	

Note: Dried wisteria vines and edgeworthia can be reshaped after they have been soaked in deep water for a few hours. For modern and dramatic effect, cattails and vines can be sprayed with a coat of black lacquer.

GLYCERIN METHOD

Acuba	Chinese Hawthorn	Mahonia
Aralia	Cycas Fern Palm	Nandina
Aspidistra	Euonymus	Pandanus
Barberry	Galax	Scotch Broom
Beech	Grape Ivy	Ti
Birch	Leather Leaf	Wild Huckleberry
Boxwood	Lemon	Yucca
Camellia	Magnolia	

Note: Ground foliage, such as ivy, can be submerged in glycerin solution for about four days. It will turn a pleasing shade of olive green. After the treatment, rinse the glycerin off the leaves with cool water. A coat of clear lacquer spray will add to the sheen and protection of foliage.

Dried materials can be arranged with a flair if you put your imagination to use. For instance, they can be combined with fresh flowers, dried interesting branches, or driftwood.

In PLATE 33 compatible textures are brought together with a whirling wisteria vine wrapped around a brown pottery vase from which emerge glycerin-treated mahonia branches and fresh yellow chrysanthemums.

Radiating lines of Scotch broom made supple through glycerin spread across a brown pottery container in PLATE 34. A colorful mass of orange, yellow, and red sky rockets gives strong emphasis to the design. The broom and sky rockets are secured in clusters by florist wire so they remain firm in a mound of clay.

Tall blades of New Zealand flax in *Figure* 41 acquired a mellow texture by the glycerin treatment. They rise in staggered heights with wispy Italian wheat flaring out in the background. Tiny brown pebbles, which blend with the tawny pottery compote, conceal the needlepoint holder.

In *Figure* 42 knotted New Zealand flax, bronzed by glycerin, lose their identity in a modern effect with bleached Scotch broom and fresh red anthuriums. White streaks in the brown porcelain compote reflect the same white tones of the broom.

Figure 41. New Zealand flax combines with Italian wheat flaring out from a tawny pottery compote.

Figure 42. The glycerin-treated leaves merge with bleached Scotch broom and fresh red anthuriums in a brown porcelain compote streaked with white.

Glycerin-preserved cycas fern palms, with one side completely stripped, are looped to repeat a similar circle in the stoneware aquamarine vase in *Figure 43*. Loops are made by tying the tip and base of each stem with florist wire. Fresh red gladioli arranged in a cluster, and secured in a needlepoint holder, add vivacity to this modern creation.

In *Figure 44* jet black cattails with their narrow blades, tall and slender, are in contrast to a low mass of red sky rockets. To accentuate the design, black sand covers the needlepoint holders and drifts to meet the edge of the red and black containers.

The same cattails are used in *Figure 45* with a curved wisteria vine sprayed black. A feeling of airiness and movement is conveyed by the narrow leaves which float around rigid cattails; both emerge from the open loop of the vine. Fleecy baby's breath, placed low, provides additional openness to the strong textured materials. The container is a Chinese red porcelain bowl, and for contrast, black sand blankets the needlepoint holder.

The versatile wisteria vine is used again in an upward swing to encircle three black cattails in *Figure 46*. Red and white sky rockets, which provide texture and color, are massed low in a white opaque compote to conceal the needlepoint holder.

Fluffy heads of buff-toned teasel, with natural curved stems, add striking impact to the design of *Figure 47*. Combined with strong tawny lines of lythrum, teasel blossoms radiate depth and movement from the mellow bronze bowl; the whole is sparked by brilliant orange and yellow sky rockets.

Teasel blossoms in *Figure 48* become a dominant note with auracaria, more expressively called the "monkey puzzle tree." Its short stalk with long serpentine stems dotted black and brown encircles the jet black compote.

The same auracaria stalk changes its undulating form in the tall black vase of *Figure 49*. The curved stems spiral upward to embrace teasel blossoms arranged in varying heights and directions. (These are the same flowers used in *Figures 47–48*.)

Buff-toned artichoke heads, massed in a ball, lend textural appeal to the long forceful line of driftwood balanced on a burnished amber compote in *Figure 50*. A similar buff tone is carried out in the short-stemmed spoons, staggered in the back to create an all-round view. A mound of clay supports the materials.

In *Figure 51* two peeled edgeworthia branches give the illusion of continuous rhythm swirling around a tall blue porcelain vase. They reflect the buff tones of the artichoke heads, which are placed in extreme heights. Clusters of blue sky rockets repeat the color of the swirl vase. The materials are balanced by a cross-support.

Edgeworthia creates an open lyric quality for tall stark thistles and a bed of dock in *Figure 52*. The branch follows the curved rim of the porcelain amber compote and sweeps upward in an oval loop. It is secured behind the dock in a mound of clay.

The gossamer texture of raw silk is stretched tautly over peeled edgeworthia branches, which balance each other in the pale green stoneware vase of *Figure 53*. Dried black sunflowers, supported in a clay mound, create a vibrant mood for this modern design of subtle contrasting textures.

Dried pussy willows create airiness and motion as they flare out from a clay mound to encircle large cecropia leaves in *Figure 54*. A fluttering mass of bright orange sky rockets is added for accent to enhance the black mottled compote.

A symphony of autumn tones is brought together in this natural composition shown in *Figure 55*. Stark yarrow stems and soft swaying heads of barley, supported in a needlepoint holder, rise from an amber porcelain compote.

A Chinese philosopher in *Figure 56* appears to be enjoying a leisurely stroll in a woodland atmosphere of palm spathes and tall sprays of buckwheat that rise from a burl slab. Clusters of yarrow and yucca pods are combined with rocks and small stones to conceal the clay mound, and to add realism to the composition.

Figure 43. Fresh red gladioli combine with cycas fern palms looped to repeat a similar circle in the aquamarine stoneware vase.

Figure 44. Cattails provide dramatic effects. The jet black is in contrast to the red sky rockets in red and black containers.

Figure 45. Narrow leaves float around black cattails, which emerge from the loop of black lacquered wisteria vine. Baby's breath provides airiness to the design. The container is Chinese red porcelain.

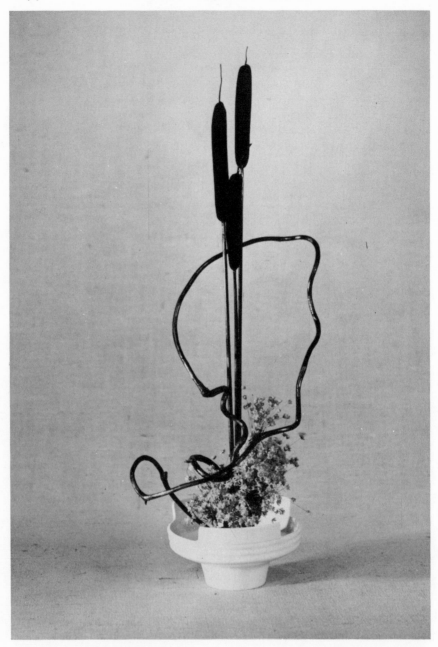

Figure 46. Wisteria vine is used again in an upward swing to encircle black cattails with red and white sky rockets massed low in a white opaque compote.

Figure 47. Unlimited possibilities with teasel. These buff-toned blossoms radiate depth and movement for strong lines of lythrum in a bronze-colored bowl, accented by orange and yellow sky rockets.

Figure 48. Teasel here becomes the dominant note, with auracaria, whose short stalk with serpentine stems encircles the black compote.

Figure 49. The same auracaria stalk changes its undulating form in a tall black vase. The curved stems spiral upward to embrace varying heights of teasel blossoms.

Figure 50 (above). Effects with artichokes and edgeworthia. Buff-toned artichoke heads are massed low with spoons against a forceful line of driftwood in an amber compote.

Figure 51 (right). Peeled edgeworthia branches swirl around a blue porcelain vase which holds artichoke heads and blue sky rockets.

Figure 52. Edgeworthia creates an open lyric quality for tall stark thistles and a bed of dock in an amber compote.

PLATE 31. This carefully artless arrangement of geraniums enhances the natural beauty of the flowers. The understated basket container gives texture contrast.

PLATE 32. The circular motif is consistent in this centerpiece arrangement of orange snowballs in a color-matched pottery bowl.

PLATE 33. A whirling wisteria wrapped around a pottery vase combines with glycerin-treated mahonia and fresh chrysanthemums.

PLATE 34. Radiating lines of glycerinized Scotch broom spread across a pottery compote, with emphasis on massed sky rockets.

PLATE 35. Deep orange tapers highlight this low arrangement of carnations and dracaena.

PLATE 36. The tall pottery container transforms the same carnation-dracaena design into a completely different arrangement.

PLATE 37. Plastic water lilies and their pads create a deceptive "fresh" centerpiece in a glass bowl.

PLATE 38. Dried pussy willows are looped in an outline for artificial tulips in a porcelain container on a sun-shaded patio table.

PLATE 39. Amber-colored roses, which reflect the same shade in the pottery plate, follow the flat ferns in a centerpiece placed on a drop-leaf table.

PLATE 40. Multicolored anemones lend charm to this double composition in a pair of lacquer containers.

Figure 53. Raw silk of filmy texture is stretched over edgeworthia which balance each other in a pale green stoneware vase. Dried black sunflowers contrast effectively.

Figure 54. Dried pussy willows encircle cecropia leaves and bright orange sky rockets in a black mottled porcelain compote.

Figure 55. A symphony of autumn tones is brought together in this natural composition with yarrow and soft heads of barley. Container is amber-colored porcelain.

Figure 56. A Chinese philosopher appears to be enjoying a leisurely stroll in this woodland atmosphere.

CHAPTER 7

Flowers That Last and Last

Artificial flowers and foliage are now available at most florists and department stores in many species and in a spectrum of colors. They range from garden flowers to exotic tropical plants. Those of better quality have a life-like appearance. Although they lack the fragrance of growing plants, their permanence and endless variety are a boon for anyone with little access to freshly cut flowers and foliage.

With imagination and careful planning, artificial flowers can be arranged artistically either alone or combined with dried or fresh materials. Here are some ideas:

On hot summer days introduce an atmosphere of coolness with simulated water-growing plants floating in a shallow bowl. Such a design is refreshing for a dining or coffee table.

The rich fall tones of permanent plants, when merged with natural textures of driftwood or rugged barks, can create realistic compositions.

During the somber months of winter when flowers are scarce, combine the warm colors of artificial flowers with fresh evergreens.

While flowers are plentiful in the spring, artificial evergreens sometimes add a nice touch without their being obvious.

Using artificial flowers and foliage has many advantages. Because of their flexible stems they bend to any shape and take on an astonishing likeness to nature. They require a little skill, but they keep indefinitely. The simpler the design the more appeal. Arrangements can be worked out in advance, dismantled, stored, then reassembled when the need arises.

Artificial flowers have a resilient nature and are heavier than live ones. They are best supported in a metal or plastic cage holder filled with clay. To secure the holder to a shallow container, press a strip of clay around it. A suction base holder or a small mound of clay will support lightweight stems. Clay can be reused by kneading until it becomes pliant. Also available commercially is a hard set clay which will keep an arrangement indefinitely, but once set it cannot be removed.

When fresh and artificial materials are combined, a needlepoint holder should be used. Since most artificial stems are too resilient for this type of holder, the stem should be bound to a short woody stem for easy insertion.

Heavy wire clippers will cut artificial stems; if the severed end is rough, bind it with florist tape to prevent marring the container. By removing some of the blossoms and foliage from an evenly distributed spray, a floral design becomes more interesting. Save these single flowers or leaves to fill open gaps in the base of an arrangement.

A plastic flower head can be reshaped by dipping it into boiling water for several seconds until the petals soften. Remove it immediately and tighten or loosen the petals, then place the flower head under cold running water to set it firmly.

Keep artificial flowers away from heated areas and strong sunlight. Heat of any kind will soften the clay and relax its grip on the stems; sunlight will fade the color.

To give your arrangement a fresh look, spray with a mist bath of cool water. Daily spraying will also remove accumulated dust from plastic plants. For a thorough cleaning, use warm soapy water, then rinse in cold water.

PLATES 35–36 show two entirely different arrangements using the same floral materials. The clump of leaves was individually stapled to form loose loops, then inserted in a mound of clay. In varying low heights, five carnations were tied with florist wire to form a tight mass in contrast to the looped foliage.

Arranged as a centerpiece in a greenish-brown earthenware plate, the dracaena and carnations are complemented by the deep orange candles.

As a vase design, the rich luminous textures of dracaena and carnations interrelate with the modern tan pottery container placed on a mahogany table in a library setting.

Dried wisteria vines make a graceful framework for artificial flowers and create movement with no break in rhythm. An example is shown in *Figure 57* using a gourd-shaped pottery container with two openings. The tones are grayish-green. Three red carnations of varying heights are balanced securely in the small top opening, and four shorter ones, supported in a cage holder, emerge from the lower opening.

Figure 58 illustrates an interesting combination using fresh, dried, and artificial materials. Dried black wisteria tendrils float around a large artificial yellow dahlia framed by fresh leather ferns in a black porcelain compote. The arrangement is on a marble coffee table.

Another example is expressed in *Figure 59*. Fresh wisteria branches combine with artificial blue Dutch irises and pine sprays in a landscape effect. Two rocks of different shapes add interest to the ivory-colored porcelain container. (Iris and pine stems were joined separately to fresh woody stems for easy insertion in the needlepoint holder.)

A mirrored base in *Figure 60* reflects two black cranes who seem to enjoy the woodland of soft green ferns and pink clusters of geraniums growing amid rocks.

Two mounds of clay, placed on extreme sides of the mirror, support the materials. Rocks of different shapes form banks for the ferns and geraniums and help to conceal the mechanics.

The theme for this luncheon table appointment in PLATE 37

is a water scene in pastel. Pale pink water lilies and their pads float in a green glass bowl to create a refreshing atmosphere. The three groups are placed in small suction holders; two long slender stems, tucked under the foliage, give a feeling of natural growth. Tiny pebbles drift into the pond-like open water.

The natural, combined with the artificial, becomes a centerpiece for a sun-shaded patio table in PLATE 38. Fresh pussy willows bound individually with florist wire at tip and base make a circular outline for the parrot tulips massed low in the center. Sprays of cypress, added for depth, conceal the cage holder in a narrow black porcelain container.

Amber-colored roses in PLATE 39 follow the directional movement of flat ferns in a wide pottery plate placed on a drop-leaf table. The color of the plate reflects the amber tones of the roses. For firm support the ferns and roses were individually bound with florist wire to a short sturdy stem.

In PLATE 40 bright-colored anemones lend charm to a double composition in twin red lacquer containers. The flowers unite harmoniously into a compositional unity. Clay mounds, which support the anemones, are concealed by short foliage.

Figure 57. Dried wisteria vines make graceful frameworks for artificial red carnations in a gourd-shaped pottery grayish-green vase with two openings.

Figure 58. A large artificial dahlia is framed by fresh leather ferns in a black porcelain compote.

Figure 59. Fresh wisteria branches create a naturalistic effect with artificial Dutch irises and pine sprays in an ivory-colored porcelain container.

Figure 60. A mirrored base reflects two ebony cranes who seem to enjoy a woodland atmosphere amid a rocky bank.

Index

ACKNOWLEDGMENTS

The following photographs appeared in color in *Family Circle* magazine, and were taken by George Nordhausen:

Plates 1–4, 6, 10–12, 15–21, 24–26, 28–32, 35–40; Figures 2–3, 13, 24, 27–28, 30–31, 36–37, 41.

Other credits are, William A. Carr for Plates 3, 7–9, 13–14, 22–23, 33–34; Figures 4–12, 14–23, 25–26, 29, 32–35, 38–40, 42–60.

Plates 5 and 27, and Figure 1 by permission of Kikkoman International.

28-019122

| NOV 2 1976 | DATE DUE |

PLEASE KEEP THIS
CARD IN BOOK POCKET

A CHARGE OF 25¢ WILL
BE MADE IF CARD IS
MUTILATED OR LOST

GREENBURGH
PUBLIC LIBRARY

300 TARRYTOWN ROAD
ELMSFORD, N.Y. 10523

IF REQUIRED
FOLD HERE BEFORE PLACING IN POCKET